Twelve Rules for Getting Rich

Avant® Leadership
Guide Series

Twelve Rules for Getting Rich

Dynamic Secrets of Financial Success

Christopher Scott

Avant Books®
San Marcos, California

Library of Congress Catalog Card Number 90-53174

ISBN 0-932238-52-1

Avant Books®
Slawson Communications, Inc
San Marcos, California 92060-1436

Printed in the United States

Interior Design by Sandy Mewshaw

Artwork Estay Heustis

1 2 3 4 5 6 7 8 9 10

Table of Contents

About the Author

The author holds a Ph.D. in economics and has been a professor of Finance and Real Estate at several large universities.

He has fifteen-years experience as the owner of a financial consulting firm, has headed up numerous real estate development investment groups, and is a lecturer throughout the west on negotiating and financing techniques.

To all those who have helped me learn from their experience
and to all those who may learn from mine.

Introduction

> *This Book is Different:*
> *Make Money Your Way*

So many of the advice books and seminars today try and suggest that their way is the best or only way to get rich. Buy Options! Sell Real Estate! Clean Carpet! Invest in Mutuals! And on, and on.

The truth is, that while these avenues might work for those individuals who **enjoy** working and studying in each of those fields, they will do little for those with no interest in the product or activity. The authors and seminar leaders give examples of people who have made large sums of money by following their plans. What they neglect to mention is that those folks were almost assuredly interested in the subject and enjoyed the work.

Of all the traits common to financial success stories, nothing is more important than the fact that the men and women involved decided to *make money by doing what they enjoy* rather than trying to enjoy what they were doing. They took an idea which excited them and, because of their enthusiasm and interest, the hours passed quickly, chores became achievements and at some point they prospered.

The real shame is that most people fail to recognize what should be obvious: fortunes have always been made and will continue to be made in *every field* imaginable. There is *no one single road* to riches.

Look at a very brief list of men and women who have made fortunes, and their chosen fields: Onassis-shipping, Walton-retailing, Rubenstein-cosmetics, Cardin-fashion, and Marriott-hotels. All had different backgrounds, nationalities and education. Suffice it to say that their fields of interest are as diverse as possible. I'm sure they all worked hard but, unlike the majority of workers, they enjoyed the work because their ideas were born from a love of what they were doing. Interest and enthusiasm were the parents and financial rewards were the offspring.

After years of associating with men and women who have made their own fortunes, it has become clear that there are certain common *rules* which guide their actions and decisions. In conversations about how they manage their money and business, the same basic ideas kept popping up, regardless of how their money was made. Not all of the rules are followed all of the time, but it's surprising how often they are followed and how much thought is given before deviating from them.

A reading of financial history, and the lives of the people who made the most impact, suggests that the rules haven't changed in hundreds or thousands of years. The secrets of acquiring and keeping wealth were about the same in ancient Greece as they are in contemporary New York. The following pages set out, and briefly discuss, some of the most common and important of these *rules*. I'm sure there are others that have particular applications, but these should provide enough food for thought to get started. They are time-tested and experience-proven.

Your ideas can work, too. There will be problems and disappointments, but that's true when you are working at a job you don't like for wages that will never make you rich. Despite popular opinion, the problems of a job you don't like are the challenges and achievements of a project you love.

Think about the *rules* and how they apply to you. They will help you to achieve financial security and the time to enjoy it with family and friends.

Rule 1

Words Mechanics Hate to Hear:
"I Took It Apart Myself and
Everything's in the Bucket.
You Just Have to Put It Together."

Do One Thing Very Well

Leonardo de Vinci was the exception and not the rule, *the true renaissance man*, artist, sculptor, inventor, scientist, and engineer. Unfortunately, few of us will ever excel at such a variety of endeavors. Once we accept that fact, the question is *should we even try to do everything ourselves?* There are books, video tapes and classes covering just about everything from repairing your car's transmission to installing carpet and programming computers. They all advertise how much money and time you can save by doing it yourself. The truth is, except for the occasional instance, it's not true. Sure, if a bolt needs tightening in your washing machine to stop it from vibrating across the room, and you know how to fix it, and it takes only a short time, go ahead and do it. In terms of your financial success and security, however, it doesn't justify more than a few minutes of your time; unless you enjoy fixing appliances more than anything else, and if so—why aren't you doing it full time?

Think of the financially successful people you either know, know of, or read about. One of the characteristics that most of them have in common is devotion and committment to one activity. Furthermore, it's almost always what they enjoy doing most. This explains why they do it so well and, consequently, why they make money in the process.

In fact, most financially successful individuals are highly *focused*; that is, they appear obsessed by the work they do. Isn't it far better to **want** to work hard because you love what you are doing, rather than endure doing things you don't enjoy? I always hear people say that the *rich* guy down the street works twelve hours a day. Well, most of us work long hours. The difference is that the *rich* guy works his hours doing what he does best, and therefore very profitably, while his neighbor works at a job he doesn't care about and spends the rest of his time repairing his dishwasher in order to save the repair bill.

Both people work the same hours, but as time passes the financial rewards of the person doing one thing very well far surpasses the other. Moreover, and perhaps most importantly, not only does that person make much more money, but he has a lot more fun, and more leisure time to do the other things he enjoys and can afford. None of this is to imply that you can't have, or shouldn't have, hobbies and a variety of interests in addition to your work. It is a matter of priorities.

Financially secure people have become financially secure by doing what they enjoy most and fully committing their energy to it—which is surprisingly easy since their work is fun! If you are a produce manager and find that your working hours are spent thinking about the cars you are restoring in your garage, and enthusiastically rush there to work until midnight, then it's time to make a serious effort to change jobs and work for a firm that restores cars. You'll work with joy and go overboard to do well; your reputation will grow and so will your financial rewards. You'll also be enjoying full time what you previously could only afford as a hobby. Your time with your family will be better spent and you'll be able to afford to hire someone else to paint the house.

- Think about what you really want to do.

- Financial success will be yours if you do it very well.

- To do it very well, put aside other chores and concentrate your energy and enthusiasm on what you do best.

Rule 2

> *Famous Las Vegas Saying:*
> *"I'll Be Back in an Hour Honey,*
> *I Just Want to Get Even."*

Cut Losses

When I was about thirteen-years-old my uncle, who enjoyed visiting the race track, took me with him one day. In fact, I was too young to be admitted and it must have looked comical when my uncle, who is over six feet tall, gave me his sports coat and told me to buy a ticket at the entry gate. I had to pull up the sleeves of his jacket about a foot in order for my hands to stick out, and I think the only reason they let me in was because the cashier couldn't stop laughing.

I didn't know a lot about betting on horses, and after three or four races the ten dollars I had brought was gone. I went to my uncle and asked if he would loan me two dollars. He asked why I needed the loan. I told him that I wanted to get even. He looked at me and said "If you wanted to get even, you should have stayed at home. You were even before we came." This well-learned lesson has been been repeated time and time again.

The objective of any business transaction, the objective of making money, the objective of most things we do, is not to get even, but to progress. Yet, after suffering losses, how many of us have decided to remain in the deal until we get even? If you are one who has done that, think back and ask yourself, "Did I ever get even?" If you did, how hard was it? How much time did it take? Could you have better used your time doing something that had more potential profit right from the start?

Obviously there are businesses and ventures that require start up periods when profits are non-existent or small. Pharmaceutical companies, electronic firms and others, have heavy research and development costs, and time expectations before profits can be made. The difference is whether or not financial losses and time run-overs are anticipated at the outset. The mistake made by many is to expect a profitable business from the beginning. Then the error is compounded by pursuing the venture, allowing it to lose more time and money than the project deserves.

Historically, some ventures have succeeded after sustaining heavy losses, but most individuals don't have large supplies of capital to invest. When the amount that can be comfortably lost has been lost, it is time to stop and consider if minor adjustments will correct the problem or if the entire venture was a mistake. And, if it was a mistake, should you stop, accept your losses, and get on with something else? There have been instances when an entrepreneur has closed a business and, drawing on experience, reopened a similar business successfully.

In most cases however, people wait far too long before admitting that things aren't going well. There is an old saying, "You'll never go broke making a profit, even if it's small." The converse of that is, "You'll never make a profit if you keep losing money, no matter how little you continually lose."

My partner and I once bought a house in Sacramento, California, as an investment. We thought we had a terrific deal. The house had been part of a property settlement in a divorce. It was a large house in a moderately expensive neighborhood and the wife, now ex-wife, could not afford to make the payments. She called us and asked if we would be interested in purchasing the house. Her ex-husband had built it when they were married the first time. They were later divorced and the husband retained the house. He remarried, divorced his second wife, and continued to retain the house. He then remarried his first wife and when they were divorced the second time, she wound up with the house. Perhaps we should have known then that this was no ordinary house. In any event, we bought it for what we thought was at least thirty thousand under market value and put the house up for sale.

After three months we had not had one offer. Four months later we still had none. We finally decided that the interior needed some redecorating. Six months after the improvements were made we still hadn't had an offer. We decided to rent the property in order to produce a cash flow to help with the house payments. In a matter of several weeks a couple lease-optioned the property, but two weeks later the man died and the woman moved out, and we had the house on the market again. Finally, at a real estate meeting, we mentioned our house to an acquaintance who owned a Cessna Aircraft dealership. He looked at us as if we were crazy and proceeded to tell us that we just didn't know how to market the property and that he could surely get rid of the house and make a profit in no time at all.

That's all we needed to hear and thirty minutes later we had exchanged our equity in the house (which we recognized was rapidly diminishing each month we made a payment) for his equity in a brand new airplane. We actually had some use for the plane as we were both pilots.

About nine months later we ran into our friend at another meeting and noticed that he made no mention of the house. We stood the suspense as long as possible and finally asked how he had done with the house. He laughed, asked how we were enjoying the airplane and wanted to know if we would like to consider reversing the trade. He hadn't had an offer on the house—not one offer—since our trade with him. This was some years ago and for all I know the house remains vacant.

The point is, we would have been better off had we reduced the price of the house by thirty thousand dollars as soon as it became evident that it was not going to sell quickly. We could have given the deed back to the lender, or done anything else we could have thought of. Our plan had been for a quick profit and when that plan was not realized we should have taken action to cut our losses.

Not *biting the bullet* soon enough is probably the single, most-prevalent failing I see among self-employed investors and business people. This doesn't mean you must close your business or that you have failed, it simply means that you have recognized that some things work and some things don't, and you should expend your efforts on those which make profits.

Good business people who have made fortunes have not made them by throwing good money after bad for very long. Admitting that one venture or one idea is not as good as you thought is not an admission of failure. If you own a restaurant and have lima beans as the special and don't sell any lima beans, you can still continue to operate your restaurant, but perhaps you should change your vegetable of the day.

When I first went to work for a Wall Street investment banking firm, one of the partners of the firm handled a great many discretionary accounts; that is, accounts in which people had entrusted money to be invested without requiring their approval on each and every transaction. About a year after I joined the firm the market took a serious turn for the worse and people were losing money right and left, but this one partner seemed to be doing okay—not great, but making money in the face of a declining market and in the face of other experts' losses.

After bribing him with an expensive lunch I could ill afford, I brought up the matter and asked for his sage advice. I expected a long discourse on investment strategy, the fundamentals of the market place, technical analysis, the random walk thesis, and all sorts of other academic approaches to money. Instead, this man, who was quite wealthy in his own right, took one last bite of his chocolate mousse pie and said, "When a piece of junk that I own goes down a quarter of a point I sell it and buy another piece of junk that's going up a quarter of a point. Thanks for lunch, goodbye." At the time I wasn't quite sure the advice was worth the sixty-dollar lunch, but I came to realize it was worth far more than that. In fact he and my uncle had told me the same thing. *Cut your losses and let your profits run.*

The hard part is admitting to having made a mistake, and admitting that the current investment or project isn't working. Don't take it personally, it happens to every millionaire and billionaire. Perhaps the biggest single difference between them and the rest of the world is that they act quickly to recognize and rectify their mistakes. It's no fun losing, and getting even is only slightly better. Remember, allowing losses to continue means that, from that point on, your energy will be spent getting back to even, and you were even before you started.

Rule 3

> *Getting to the Core of the Matter*

A Financial Strategy That Works

Not too many years ago, companies went on a buying spree and bought other companies. The theory was diversification or synergism, which advocated that the whole could be greater than the sum of its parts. At about the same time, students coming out of the MBA program at Harvard were led to believe that, essentially, all businesses were run the same way. Further, with a good enough degree you could step out of the classroom and successfully run a steel mill, an automobile factory, a flower shop, an investment banking firm, or any other business. The years since have disproved the idea of synergism. In fact, and this is consistent with our point of view of doing one thing well, most highly-successful businesses or investors have concentrated the bulk of their attention on what they do best.

This is not to suggest that branching out is foolhardy, but there is a way to diversify and a way to expand into other endeavors without jeopardizing the profits, income, cash flow, and security, that provided the money to branch out. In order to define this better, let's call it the *core approach*. It looks something like this:

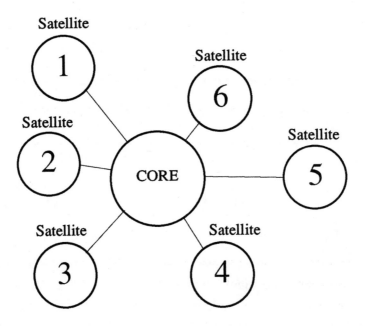

Figure 3-1

The large circle in the middle represents the basis of your business or investment activities. In other words, it represents the primary concentration of your energy. It is the thing you do best, the thing you rely on for day-in and day-out profits. Even more importantly, it is the activity that receives the most attention, and the activity that must continue to grow at a satisfactory rate. The core is the first and foremost activity in importance.

Stated differently, this is the source of all income, both necessary and discretionary, and it is the engine which feeds and runs any other activities. Nearly all highly-successful businesses have become successful by paying attention to one primary enterprise. Nearly all great investors have always had one investment vehicle to which they paid the most consistent attention and to which they retreated in difficult times. If and when things got bad, the investors regrouped around that one particular strategy that first made them profitable.

What people tend to forget is that the core must continue to grow in order to provide the means to undertake other enterprises or investments, which we will call satellites. The practical approach is really fairly simple. As the core grows at whatever rate is appropriate (and it should be a realistic and relatively predictable rate), some of the funds generated are reinvested in the core itself to keep it growing. Of the remainder some are set aside for reserves and the balance is available for funding satellite investments.

The important thing to understand is that the satellites are interesting intellectual and financial diversions, but they are not what puts food on the table and a Rolls Royce in the garage. That remains the job of the core. If the satellite does well, so much the better. If it doesn't it's probably best to cut the losses quickly and not drain good money from the core to chase bad money in the satellite.

There can be any number of satellites, usually some do well and some not so well. The most common mistake is to allow the tail to wag the dog; or, in this case the satellite to dictate policy at the expense of the core.

Usually this occurs when the investor or businessman refuses to admit that the satellite is a loser while he continues pumping more time, energy and resources into it. He thereby debilitates the core as well as other satellites.

Furthermore, because people are hesitant to admit that they have made a mistake, or because they are hesitant to accept the loss (at least psychologically), they don't shut down the satellite soon enough. More than one company, and more than one individual, have gone under because they took from the good to feed the bad. In the early seventies, the executives of many companies thought that successfully running their core business gave them the ability to run other businesses equally well and their sustaining business core paid the price. They learned in fairly short order that each business is truly different.

Even though there are well-established principles applicable to all businesses, there are also specialized skills needed. These skills can usually be acquired only through *on the job* experience.

To summarize and conclude, highly successful businesses and investors usually concentrate on one primary activity which we have called the core. They reinvest proceeds from the core back into the core to assure its continued growth and health. They then use some of the remaining funds to finance other investments, businesses, or activities, with the understanding that everything possible will be done to make the satellites work. If the satellites fail, the managers will cut their losses and try another satellite, or strategically retreat to their core activities until the lost funds have been restored.

Perhaps one of the morals of experience is that diversification does not necessarily provide security; the best security is provided by doing one thing very well and concentrating on building that into a strong healthy enterprise.

Rule 4

> *Jaguars and Chevrolets*
> *are Different—Chevrolets Run*

Rationalizing Good and Bad Decisions

Strange title for a chapter? Not really. Let me explain: I have two cars—a Jaguar and a Chevrolet El Camino. I have heard many Jaguar owners defend their ownership by discussing the cars' value, engineering, comfort, and a variety of other attributes. (The fact that they feel a need to mount a defense should tell you something.) The truth of the matter is, as all Jaguar owners know, the car spends an enormous amount of time in the shop, its resale value is less than other cars in terms of percentage of total cost, and insurance costs are unbelievable.

My Chevy, on the other hand, cost about a third as much, starts every day, requires almost no maintenance, retains its resale value, has a reasonable insurance cost and, by any rationale criteria, makes far more sense to own. Why then do I, and a number of other so-called enthusiasts, own Jaguars? The plain and simple truth is they make us feel good; they make us feel important, wealthy, attractive, impressive to others, and whatever other adjectives you might care to add. The interesting part is that we seldom admit this *out loud*, preferring to rationalize our ownership under the guise of engineering, investment, and a lot of other nonsense. Why don't we just admit the real reason and get on with enjoying the car, boat, jacuzzi or whatever it is that we are working so hard to justify on objective terms?

Unfortunately, I don't really know the answer, but I do know that a great many poor business decisions are made in much the same way. An earlier discussion talked about cutting losses. Justifying the continuance of bad decisions is a closely-related issue. The most common occurrence surfaces when one aspect of a business is performing poorly and we allow our egos to become involved, particularly if we were originally responsible for the activity. This may happen even if the losing idea is performing poorly because of management problems, marketing problems, or simply being a good idea at the wrong time or place.

Mae West said that when she was good she was very good and when she was bad she was better. Wish it were so. One thing that successful people have told me, again and again, is that most of their really successful endeavors have been good right from the start. They have problems, to be sure, but they have continually moved forward from day to day. They also admit that very few bad endeavors have been turned around. There are always stories in *Forbes, Fortune,* and the *Wall Street Journal,* about individuals who took over a failing business and made it into a great enterprise. In reality, most bad ideas are never turned around and the folks who have reversed one business often find, to their dismay, that they cannot perform the same miracle on the next problem. More than one turnaround artist has been disillusioned and found their ego badly bruised on subsequent tries.

If, by chance, you have turned around a failing business and made it prosper, my suggestion is to declare yourself a hero for all time and never try it again —your place in history will be secure. What we know from an empirical observation is that good investments don't usually go bad, and bad investments hardly ever become good.

Separate your personal wants from your business needs. If you really want the $5,000 teakwood desk, make the decision to purchase it apart from the rationalization that it will impress your customers. Don't kid yourself that you want the desk, car, or airplane for the best interest of the business when you really want it to make yourself feel good. Also, don't destroy a good investment by siphoning off the profits to support a poor one. Each business activity should stand on its own merit.

Rule 5

```
Nothing Down?
P.T. Barnum is Alive and
Well and Lives in a Seminar Hall
```

Debt and Liquidity

Perhaps you have read the books, attended the seminars, or seen the advertisements on television. You know the ones I mean—How to buy property with no money down—How to acquire ten million dollars of property in six months with nothing down—No down payment.

Sounds great, doesn't it! Let me give you some background, and use it to illustrate the general principle. Between 1978 and 1983, if you recall, interest rates in the United States and other places in the world sky-rocketed. The prime rate exceeded 16%, treasury bills were yielding unheard of returns, and in general, interest rates were at near historical highs. Consequently, it became very difficult to sell real property—apartments, homes, commercial real estate, and all the rest. Many of the properties had adjustable rate mortgages and the owners couldn't afford to make the payments. Further, because of lease arrangements they couldn't raise rents (and even if they could, in the face of even a minor recession, tenants could not have afforded to pay the increases).

Consequently, a great deal of property was for sale, but potential buyers couldn't afford to finance at the high interest rates any better than the current owners. The upshot was that streets were lined with *For Sale* signs and real estate brokers and agents, except for the few well-established ones, were looking for other lines of work. The principal motivation of many property owners, who had some equity, was to sell the property rather than lose money each month. The risk of ultimate foreclosure was also very real.

Along came a group of slick investors who offered to buy the property for nothing down in exchange for taking over the owners' payments. For their equity, owners received notes secured by mortgages or deeds of trust. Many sellers accepted this deal, motivated by the real fear of being unable to make payments. The problem was that the new owners weren't any better qualified to make the payments than the old ones, and it wasn't long thereafter that these new buyers defaulted on both the bank payments and their notes to the sellers.

This forced the seller to take back the property in order to protect whatever remaining equity there was. The process of taking back the property was costly, time consuming, and further eroded much of whatever equity existed in the property.

Proponents of the no-money down technique would tell you that they had acquired one, two or five million dollars worth of property in a very short time and were on their way to financial security. One woman at a seminar stood up and said that she had acquired fifteen million dollars worth of commercial property in only six months and that she could make $200,000 if she sold it within the next year. A $200,000 profit in one year on a fifteen million dollar investment is less than a two percent annual return. It could be far greater if her investment was minimal (leveraged). However, it's easy to figure that the loans on the acquired property were nearly fifteen million, and at high interest rates, $200,000 of equity can quickly disappear in monthly payments.

Moreover, there was no mention of selling costs, no mention of commissions to be paid, no mention of concessions that might be required to get a buyer, and no mention of any other costs associated with holding the property. Most importantly, assuming this woman took over the loans on the property, she was obligated to repay a debt of nearly fifteen million dollars (or suffer whatever consequences there would be for defaulting on the loan), in exchange for a $200,000 profit. Certainly, $200,000 is nothing to sneeze at, but it is not a satisfactory return for the financial implications of incurring a fifteen million dollar liability, even if she had almost nothing invested of her own cash.

There are several points to be made here; the first is that it is relatively easy to acquire assets if you are also willing to acquire liabilities; it's easy to buy a million dollars worth of property if you are willing to accept a million dollars worth of debt or liabilities. Profit derives from equity and equity is the difference between the fair market value of an asset, less the amount owed on that asset, including the costs of holding the asset, selling the asset, and managing the asset. The people who tell you how much property they acquired should also tell you how much debt they have acquired along with it. Only then can a real determination of the potential profitability of the property be established.

The second point is that it is easier to borrow money than it is to repay it. During times when lending institutions have a lot of money to lend, their credit standards go down. They won't admit this, but it is clear that when excess funds exist there is a need to place those funds so that the institutions can earn returns. When this happens, it also becomes easier for borrowers to acquire money.

The next point is that during periods of high interest rates, it is often easy to acquire assets by taking over other peoples' debts. Along with the blessing, however, comes the curse: You have to make the payments. The time to accept debt is when interest rates are low and not when interest rates are high, even though it may be easier to make the deal because sellers may be in trouble. Borrowing money to finance investments is called leverage, and clearly the fewer of your own dollars invested in a project, the higher return on your money.

The catch, of course, is that leverage is a two-edged sword and every dollar of profit represents a high rate of return, but every dollar of deficit represents a high rate of loss. In other words, leverage is risky. It is particularly risky when interest rates are high and subject to change. If most of the earnings in your venture are used in interest payments, it doesn't take much of a rise in interest rates to wipe out what little profit existed before.

Shrewd investors—those who pay attention to trends and act on their beliefs—recognize that a rise in interest rates is a good time to liquidate assets and get into a cash position. After interest rates have risen, and the economy is in a slump, those individuals with liquidity—*real cash*—can often get bargains on property, businesses, or other investments.

Before we proceed, a word about liquidity. Many people misunderstand what liquidity really is. First of all, liquidity and value have nothing to do with the price paid for something. If you purchased stock at twenty dollars a share which is now worth twelve dollars a share the value on your balance sheet is twelve dollars, less whatever costs there are of liquidating that stock. It doesn't matter that you paid twenty dollars for it; it isn't worth that now and there's no point in kidding yourself. In measuring your liquidity, you need to measure and estimate the return you could expect today. A less conservative measure of liquidity would be to assume that you had one month, three months or six months to sell the asset.

Realistically, liquidity is how much someone would pay today, in cash, for whatever you want to market. The ultimate liquid asset is cash in your pocket, and if you want to get some true values show up with grocery bags full of cash. Turn them upside down, let the cash spill onto the table, and sit quietly while the seller looks at all that money.

The secret then is to confine borrowing to periods when interest rates are low and not be suckered into borrowing heavily in periods of high interest rates, even though the initial cash requirements of the investment are extremely low. Remember, they are low for a reason, and the reason is that the other guy can't make the payments at the high rates being charged. During periods of high rates you want to be in a cash position, either to invest in high yielding safe securities or to pick up bargains which always abound during those times. Moral—don't be lulled into incurring debt and risking your other well-secured assets when interest rates are high.

One of the secrets of financial success is having the financial ability to weather storms and to last during the hard times. The reason there were so many losses during the last period of high interest was because the payments (understand that to mean interest payments) were too high, and the owners could not hold on until the good times returned. The real shame is that they often funded those interest payments with profits from other investments acquired at more favorable terms. Because of bad judgment, they sometimes lost the good investments as well as the bad. I know about it to some degree, I was there and it won't happen again.

Rule 6

We Lose a Little on Each Deal—
But Make it Up in Volume

Buy Profits, Not Tax Losses

With recent changes in federal tax laws some of the so called tax-shelters have been eliminated. There are still, however, any number of investment schemes designed to shelter income from taxes. These range from relatively simple straightforward IRA's to more complex corporate leasing activities, as well as off-shore tax shelters.

A typical scenario might go like this: the telephone rings and the caller tells you about a terrific way to increase your tax write-offs by five, six, or even seven times the amount of your investment. It doesn't take a genius to know that the salesman is on commission, and may or may not know anything about investments or making money, or whether he has made any of these investments himself. Yet, if you hadn't done much tax planning until then, and if the call came shortly after April 15th (and the writing of a fairly large check to the IRS), and you couldn't go out and buy the new furniture you wanted, you are probably in the right frame of mind to listen to the salesman's proposal.

Without making any specific judgment about leases, cattle feeding operations, or certain real estate investments, all of which might offer large write offs or tax incentives, you should keep in mind that some of these schemes are structured only for the tax benefits. In other words, the real economic value of the investment is completely dependent upon the tax laws. If those laws were repealed or significantly altered, a wise investor would never consider the investment on its cash returns. Put differently, these are losing propositions without benefit of the tax laws.

Of the successful investors and businessmen I have met, most invest in businesses and ventures that will produce a satisfactory return without the benefit of tax breaks at all. Tax considerations are gravy and should certainly be sopped up if available, but they should not be the sole or principal reason for an investment. Tax laws change frequently and usually for the worse. There is no reason to believe that any of the tax laws in existence will remain; but then again, reason suggests there is a chance that new investment-oriented laws will be passed.

In any case, there is really no substitute for a cash return; real dollars that exist after paying debt service, principal, operating expenses, overhead, rates, taxes and all the other costs of being in business. This is the only money that is truly yours and the only money that can truly be called *profits*.

People always approach me with investment proposals that have great paper profits of one form or another. Some of them have great tax write-offs or offer a promissory note secured by thirty-four acres of swampland in a small South American country with great development potential. My standard reply is that if they can get Safeway to accept the promissory note and the tax write-offs in exchange for eggs, butter, chickens, and vegetables, I'll consider it. I'm not against tax shelters, nor am I against future returns so long as they are in addition to a predictable, or at least anticipated, real cash flow from the project or investment.

Ask yourself again and again: "Why should I do this?" "Where is the profit?" "How do I make a profit?" "How much do I make?" and, "Do I make the profit regardless of the tax consequences?" If the answer to the last question is yes, then the investment is one of perhaps several which you should seriously consider. If the answer is no, then in my opinion, it should be scratched from the list.

Nearly all of the highly-successful and financially-adroit individuals I know, demand projects which *throw off* cash because it is still the only *real* universally acceptable, spendable asset.

Rule 7

> *You Want How Much?*
> *My Brother Can Get it Wholesale*

Negotiation

A good bit of what I do for a living involves negotiating financial transactions. These negotiations involve lenders, buyers, sellers, and partners. Perhaps because I do so much negotiation, I have a biased view and place more importance on it than most people. However, when we realize that we negotiate all day every day, with business associates, husbands, wives, children, and social acquaintances, we begin to realize that the manner in which we negotiate and our point of view has a great deal to do with the way our lives progress.

I teach a negotiating seminar to real estate brokers, attorneys, and others who negotiate as an integral part of their profession. That seminar takes anywhere from four hours to two days, so this chapter about negotiation can't possibly be comprehensive. Rather, we will try and cover the highlights and point out negotiating techniques and attitudes shared by most successful negotiators and business people. Although there are many negotiating styles, ranging from the belligerent to the slyly conciliatory, good negotiators have many things in common despite their facades. Some of these recommendations may come as a surprise, but rest assured that whether you are negotiating the purchase of three dozen number-two pencils or ten-million-dollar real estate deals, nearly all first-rate negotiators adopt these principals at least most of the time.

1. Perhaps the most important is to prepare. I am continually astounded by how many competent business people walk into major negotiations without really having thought about *how* to negotiate the deal. They have thought about the numbers; they have thought about the facts, and even at times the positions involved, but they have given no thought and developed no plan about how to conduct the negotiations.

Part of the problem is that most business people envision themselves as being good negotiators. They like nothing better than to brag about the great deals they got. The real truth is that there is a significant difference between professionals and amateurs, and in a contest between a well-prepared professional negotiator and the typical shoot-from-the-hip buyer or seller, the professional always wins and often by a wide margin. Before we go into a negotiation we spend as much time as necessary preparing *how* to conduct that negotiation; including: where, when, the time of day, who should attend, what to do if such and such happens, and, perhaps most importantly, what we really want the end result to be.

I find that, time and time again, people entering a negotiation don't know what they want; they have a wish list that is usually unrealistic, but they haven't decided what they will accept, what they will offer, and what would be a satisfactory conclusion. Not having a goal makes it very hard to know when you get there. It is not that uncommon to see people turn down settlements that, upon further reflection, would have been acceptable. Sometimes we speed past an acceptable solution only to realize later that what we rejected was a better settlement than what was accepted. Like anything else, preparation pays off.

2. You have probably heard this before, but what people say and what people mean are often two different things. It is important to find out what people *really* mean. In a negotiation take the time to listen, to probe, and to learn what motivates the other side. To make a long story short, I was once called in to determine why the seller of a particular piece of property had rejected a cash offer which was more than fair, by almost any standard. Negotiations had totally broken down. The buyer's representative, an inexperienced young lady, asked if I could consult with her and the seller to learn why the deal wasn't closing. It didn't take long to establish that the seller's brother-in-law had sold a similar piece of property across the street for slightly more money than was being offered. The brother-in-law had sold for a low down payment and extended terms at a low interest rate. The all cash offer our buyer was making was far better, but emotionally the seller needed to receive at least the same price as his brother-in-law.

I suggested that her buyer raise the price to slightly above the brother-in-law's sales price and to structure the terms to contain an outrageously low interest rate, low payments, and other clauses favorable to the buyer. Once we did that, the seller accepted because he could now call his brother-in-law and tell him that he got a higher price.

An interesting point is that most inexperienced negotiators concentrate far more on the price than the terms. If you are a buyer, it is often easy to be successful by analyzing the whole offer, including terms, and coming up with a package of price and terms that is favorable to you, but enables the seller to feel good about the deal. Remember, nine out of ten people ask only about the price and the real meat of the deal is often contained elsewhere.

3. Don't negotiate for yourself. This may seem like an odd comment, but the fact is that while I am a competent negotiator for clients, my competence decreases dramatically when I negotiate for myself. I am emotionally and financially involved and tend to take the other side's comments and reactions too personally. The solution is easy; I have someone else negotiate for me. It may be one of my partners, or it may be a hired representative, but in any case it is someone who can enter the negotiation with the attitude that they really don't care whether or not they make a deal.

Of course that isn't true, but being able to adopt that attitude is perhaps the best defense against making a bad deal because of pressure. Obviously, I consult with whomever is negotiating on my behalf in order to assure that the negotiations are going in the direction we desire, but I leave the active participation to someone else. By the way, this also creates one other tremendous advantage. Everytime the other side makes a demand my representative can look them straight in the eye and say, "It sounds good to me, but I don't have the authority to make a decision until I talk to my client." After this happens a few times, the other side's demands and insistence on an immediate response diminishes, giving us more time to respond.

Nothing makes my mouth water more than to have some macho businessman inform me that he is the one with the authority, he is the one that can make the deal, and he is the one that I better pay attention to. Right then, I figure our chances of coming out ahead have just about doubled.

It is interesting to see how many really good negotiators enter the room as the second or third junior assistant and sit at the end of the table just watching and listening. Later, in conference with their own team, these people take charge, having had the luxury of being an observer, without the pressure of responding to the other side. The real power in a negotiation often sits in the quietest seat at the table. Try it sometime.

4. If negotiating was a horse race, American businessmen would win almost all the time. We have an attitude toward negotiating which is: *the sooner it is over the better, so that we can get on to more important things.* Unfortunately, the rest of the world, including *trained* American negotiators, enter the room far more patient and far more understanding, recognizing that the negotiating process can be a long, tedious, time-consuming effort. The difficulty with expecting all negotiations to be quick is that the other side, by virtue of their very patience, can wear you down, disrupt your timing, and force you into a position of having to alter other plans when things haven't gone as quickly as expected. It's probably a good idea to take whatever time you think is necessary to settle the issue, and triple it.

The negotiations to end the Vietnam War took far longer than most Americans expected they would. On the other hand, the Vietnamese had been fighting the Chinese, the French, and the Americans for what must have seemed like several lifetimes. Another few days, months, or years didn't really matter. In short, patience is a prerequisite for successful negotiations, and unless you think your position is so strong that you can simply run over your opposition, be prepared for lengthy discussions and consider the way these discussions may work to your advantage.

5. Here is a short piece of advice: when you don't understand something, stand up and say, "I don't understand." When you need time to think about something, don't hesitate to say, "We need a recess." No one can force you to remain in the room and no one should be able to force you to continue with a point that you don't understand. Interestingly enough, if you don't understand the point the other side is making, there is a good chance that they don't understand it either, and it will simply come back to haunt both sides later. Good negotiators are never afraid to admit that they have missed a point, weren't paying attention, didn't understand, or need help. Do not be intimidated by the other side's attorneys, or so-called experts. If you don't understand and need help, call time out and get your own expert, but don't be bullied.

6. Don't be predictable. By that I mean that most of us have a style which is either natural or has been developed over the years. That style typically has strengths and weaknesses, but by adopting the same negotiating style each and every time we enter discussions, the other side quickly forms a plan of attack to minimize our strengths and maximize our weaknesses. It it is hard to change a person's style; one way of dealing with this is to change negotiators. Use the tough guy when that is called for and the conciliator when that is the best approach.

This doesn't mean that each negotiator has to attend each negotiation (in fact it is sometimes more effective to have a new face show up), or that all negotiators should not attend each negotiation. It does mean that different negotiators have different roles to play, and should speak at different times on different issues. However, it should be well thought out in advance and decided which negotiator is to play which role. Keep in mind that if there is some confusion within your own group, it is time to call a recess, leave the room and discuss matters among your group.

7. Lastly, tough guys always offer ultimatums. Some take the form of take-it-or-leave-it, while others take the form of financial or business threats. My advice is two-fold: first, don't respond to ultimatums—at least not on the spot. If you are presented with an ultimatum call time out, leave the room and decide what you want to do. The ultimatum may be a bluff, or you may choose to confront the ultimatum directly and take the consequences. If someone says "Take-it-or-leave-it," you may decide to leave it because you have another supplier. If you don't have another supplier and need the product, then getting your back up and responding gruffly in the negotiation is probably not in your best interest.

Secondly, don't present ultimatums unless you are prepared to carry them out. Once you have bluffed, and not followed through, you will never again be believed. Every position you take will be suspect, and the other side will probably continue to call your bluffs until your credibility is completely undermined. On the other hand, if at times you can present an ultimatum which is not a deal-killer and you can actually follow through on it, your credibility will probably be enhanced, and subsequent strong positions are more likely to be believed. But remember, before you give ultimatums be certain that you are prepared to carry them out.

Negotiating deals can be fun, and oftentimes the real profit from a business transaction lies in how well the deal is negotiated. I strongly suggest you give it as much thought as you do the rest of your business activities.

Rule 8

How to Successfully Negotiate a Bank Loan
and Some Things to Watch For

There are any number of myths which abound in business. One of the most prevalent is that bankers know how to manage money and are good businessmen by definition. The truth is that some bankers are good businessmen and others are terrible. This has become more evident as increasing numbers of banks and savings and loans have run into serious trouble, been forced to merge with other better-managed institutions, or shut their doors. One of our most revered banking institutions has recently had its credibility tarnished because of careless loan practices and very poor management. The typical individual treats the bank as a sacred institution when, in fact, banks are businesses whose primary function is to lend money. And therein lies the secret.

Banks and other lenders must lend money if they want to stay in business, notwithstanding some of the recently proposed legislation allowing banks to become brokerage firms and engage in other direct investments. The principal source of profit for banks is the interest they earn on loans. No loans, no profits. Once this is understood, it is easy to have respect for your bank or banker without being in awe. Keep in mind, that in some sense they need you as much as you need them, even though it is a little difficult to believe when you need money.

The problem is that most people who go to a bank for a loan, particularly a business loan, have no idea what the rules of the game are, nor do they understand what the banker is looking for. I can't tell you how many times potential borrowers have walked into a bank with their idea scribbled on a napkin from yesterday's lunch, or a yellow pad with a few numbers on it, or worst of all, nothing whatsoever written down. They have a *great idea* and think the bank should loan them money just for the asking. Sorry folks, it doesn't work that way.

Here are some of the rules, written and unwritten, for gaining cooperation from a lender, that is, convincing the lender to make the loan under terms that will not guarantee failure.

Most people who go into a bank seeking a loan ask to speak to the loan officer. This next comment is a bit general, but I also believe it to be reasonably accurate. There are three kinds of loan officers: the twenty-six year old MBA in his first job who has a lending limit without supervisory approval of somewhere between fifty cents and three dollars. This loan officer won't do you any good for all the obvious reasons, and for the additional one that he doesn't yet know what he is doing.

The second kind of loan officer is in the category of those within three years of retirement. He may have been good and he may have been successful, but you can bet that he wants to go out in a blaze of glory. For bankers that means not having any problem loans, regardless of the borrowers potential for growth and profit. This type of loan officer will do almost anything to keep from rocking the boat and, consequently, will turn down your loan if your request is the least bit innovative or risky.

The third type of loan officer is probably in his late twenties to mid-thirties, has been a loan officer for a number of years and has a reasonable ($250,000) lending limit on his own authority. Also, he is ambitious and knows that the way to move up in a bank is by generating large deposits and making good loans which establish good businesses as long-term bank customers. Like other aggressive individuals, he places his own self-interest first on his list of priorities; he is usually willing to be a little more innovative and creative and accept slightly higher risks in order to produce a commendable record and hence a promotion.

The title of this chapter comes from walking into a bank with my partner and asking to see a loan officer. We were directed to a gentleman wearing a suit and white socks. I turned to my partner and said, "We don't want to make our case to anyone wearing white socks, because he has no future with the bank. As we grow we need a loan officer to grow with us. We need a loan officer whose success is tied with our success and, unless this individual has a medical reason for those socks, he's not going to move up in the bank dressed like that."

My associate thought I was exaggerating the point, but two years later that loan officer was operating a small family-owned restaurant and told me that banking is an industry that doesn't offer any opportunity. So, the first rule is to pick a banker who is as much interested in his or her personal growth as you are in yours.

The next rule is that nobody wants to take the blame for a bad loan. The manner in which lenders protect themselves against taking blame is to document their loans very, very thoroughly. A friend of mine, when going for a loan, would take what seemed like no less than ten to fifteen pounds of written material to the loan officer. Some of it may have been nothing more than Chamber of Commerce data on the number of eggs consumed per capita in their county, but when he walked into the bank he did so with a great deal of supporting material. In other words, he gave the loan officer every *justification* to *make* the loan. Furthermore, if the loan went bad, the loan officer could point to the file and say, "Gee, it had all the appearance of a good solid loan."

A very successful businessman once swore to me that he would switch banks if his banker ever actually read the information he had given to him. I'm sure this was said tongue in cheek, but his point was that lenders, like most other people in institutions, have their self-interests very near the surface, and even if they don't thoroughly read or analyze what you give them, they feel more comfortable having it available to defend favorable decisions. While the romanticized version of getting a loan may involve a deal written in pencil on a brown paper bag, the real world rarely works that way. Data, data, data. Do spread sheets, cash flows, market studies, management charts, whatever it takes to make the loan officer feel personally comfortable in making the loan. That is, if the loan should go sour, can the loan officer defend having made the loan in the first place? It is your job to see to it that he can.

The next point involves the type of loan you agree to take. Lenders always include in their loan package what are called personal guarantees and these are signed statements that you will pledge your personal assets toward repayment of the loan if the company loan goes bad. I recognize that in many cases, perhaps the vast majority of cases, the borrower will actually personally guarantee the loans. Even fairly wealthy individuals find it necessary to personally guarantee loans for their companies.

However, if there is any way it can be avoided, do so. At the very least, put up an argument and state that the value of the business is sufficient collateral. You will probably not win that argument but at the very least it will show the banker that you understand the risk of guaranteeing loans.

That brings us to another interesting point. How many times have you received mail solicitations from well-known financial companies telling you what a great credit risk you are, how confident they are of your continued success, and how, because of all this, they are willing to lend you $5,000 or $10,000 secured only by your signature? Perhaps you have been so flattered by this offer that you have even bragged to your friends and in-laws about how such and such a lender will give you money just by signing your name, no collateral necessary. Let me tell you bunky, it's a sucker play.

Given a choice of a secured or unsecured loan, always opt for the secured loan with no further guarantees. In other words, pledge some specific asset as collateral for the loan and specify that *the pledged* asset is the only collateral for the loan. The problem with unsecured signature loans is that everything you own is the collateral; everything you own is the security and the lender typically has every legal right to come after all your assets should you default. It may be flattering to have a signature loan but it's really bad business.

The next point is often neglected by borrowers. Not only does bad news travel fast, but bad news about *you* travels even faster. To the extent that bankers may understand their business, but rarely fully understand yours, any bad news—rumor or fact—that they hear about you or your business becomes a matter of exaggerated concern. The consequence is that the lender will probably overreact the way most people do when they don't have all the facts. More than likely the bad news isn't all that bad, it just seems that way to the lender when they hear it second or third hand. The way to solve this is easy—don't lie to your banker. Keep him informed and up-to-date, and if there should be some less than enthusiastic news involving yourself, your business, or your project, be certain that *you* tell your lender *first*.

Make it your business to break good news, bad news, all news, to your lender before someone else does. Very few lenders are willing to cut the string and be bad, tough guys. Think about it. When your loan is in default, that lender and that loan officer also have a loan in default. What could be stronger evidence of this than the way the largest banks in the United States have treated loans to Latin American countries over the last twenty years. Specifically, everytime one of those countries could not make an agreed upon payment, rather than carry a *bad* loan on their books (defined as a loan with interest in arrears), the bank simply loaned the borrowers enough money to make the interest payment, thereby restoring the account to a *good* loan. No bank likes bad loans. Bad loans invite regulatory audits, bad publicity, and the erosion of shareholder confidence. So long as the borrowers are honest about their difficulty and keep the lender informed, good bankers will work with them so that the loan will be repaid.

An observation: don't be overly concerned about filling out the institution's lending application. I can't believe how many times I have seen potential borrowers try and squeeze a gallon of information onto a pint size form. Typically all that the lender requires is that you sign his application and then attach all pertinent information to it. No one with any financial means can comprehensively fill out the financial statement portion that most banks provide. The form was designed by the same person who decided that bank tellers should all go to lunch between twelve and one o'clock—the exact time that everyone else is going to the bank on their lunch hour.

It is your obligation to present your case in the strongest, most attractive way possible. Don't be forced into using other people's forms or styles to do that. If the lender absolutely insists that you do it their way, they are probably not the sort of lender who is flexible enough and creative enough to do the best job for you. We have a big stamp in our office with the words *See Attached* embossed on it. No matter what form we are handed, it gets the big red stamp. We then present our case the best way we know how and staple our papers to the bank's form.

Lastly, in the past, bankers often remained with a bank for their entire career and long-lasting relationships between bank and customer were the norm. Today, banks actively raid other banks' personnel, and loan officers have no compunction about moving to other institutions and taking their good accounts with them. This may be done subtly, but the result is the same. Keep in mind that most successful borrowers aggressively shop for loans and have no hesitation about leaving their existing lender for another suitor if the terms are better.

Along the same lines, don't be intimidated by banks. Much of the intent of oak-lined offices and quiet demeanor is intended to give the bank the edge in negotiations. Don't be hesitant to present your point of view and disagree with the terms of a proposed loan. Read the loan documents carefully. They are negotiable, and it often takes many meetings with a lender to work out all the details. As a last resort, if you think you are not being treated fairly, don't hesitate to go to other lenders and make them aware that you are willing to shift your deposits to their bank, in exchange for the beginning of a new relationship. Who knows, your loan officer at the old bank may be working at the new one shortly. We're lucky to have a good, experienced and fair local banker handling our real estate developments. It took time and effort to find him, but it's been worth it.

Rule 9

> *I'll Listen to You As Soon As I'm Done Telling*
> *You What I Want to Hear*

Listening to the People Who Will
Make or Break the Deal

My favorite *Peanuts* cartoon by Charles Schulz is the one in which Lucy is walking home after school and talking to Marcy. Lucy is complaining about mathematics and how poorly she has done and Marcy keeps making suggestions about how she should study more, get a tutor, and review the homework more often. All the while Lucy is expressing how much she dislikes mathematics. Finally, after one more helpful suggestion by Marcy,

Lucy turns around and screams, "I Don't Want Solutions, I Want Sympathy!"

To the extent that generalizations are usually only half true, my opinion that there are two types of people in the world is probably half true also. I think that the point of the comic strip is that we often hear the words, but not the meaning, of people talking to us. It has been my experience that successful people are usually very good listeners. That doesn't mean they never interrupt; it means that they listen attentively for the purpose of determining the speaker's real feelings, motivations, and meanings. There was a trend in the past to carry this to the extreme and analyze beyond any reasonable measure even the most simple sentence. "I am going to the store to get a quart of milk," would bring forth a response from the social scientist or psychologist of "What I hear you saying is... " It reached the point when I felt like asking these people if English was their native tongue. "I am going to the store to get a quart of milk" meant exactly that.

However, in many other instances, meanings, shadings, and feelings, which are what people act upon, are subtly hidden among the words they say. The difficulty lies in getting people to reveal their real agenda or their real feelings without appearing to intrude or come across as abrasive and overbearing. Most people, even those we think of as being tough businessmen, seem to have a need to explain their decisions and actions. Almost invariably that explanation is rooted in emotions, biases, preconceived ideas, and cultural inheritances—far more than the individuals themselves may realize.

So, how do we listen and how do we determine what is really motivating someone, or what will motivate them, particularly if their action has an affect upon you? Consider the following scenario which, in one way or another, in one place or another, in one business or another, has been acted out innumerable times.

This example involves a real estate agent and his clients, but it could involve manufacturers, suppliers, doctors, lawyers, or shopkeepers. A couple has moved from Los Angeles, California, to Oregon for the stated purpose of getting away from people, smog, horrendous traffic, crime, and inferior schooling. They tell the agent that they wish to purchase twenty acres of ground, with or without a home, that is zoned for horses, sheep and goats, with a beautiful view, and that they have $75,000 to put down. The hard working, diligent agent spends two weeks showing the client every available large property, with and without homes, that meets the clients' description.

After spending two weeks almost exclusively with this client, the agent goes skiing with his family for the weekend, and, upon returning to the office Monday morning, calls the client to try and close a deal. The client informs the agent that just the day before, on Sunday, they purchased the cutest little home in Greenview, a subdivision of one-quarter acre parcels and tract-built homes, with a Safeway just down the street.

The agent is flabbergasted and then irritated and then angry. Finally, he hangs up the phone in disgust and tells the other agents in his office about the jerks he had for clients. The truth of the matter is that, had the agent listened actively rather than passively, the results might have been different. Most of us listen passively, but the truly good listener participates in the conversation in a subtle and yet dramatic matter. The conversation might have gone like this:

Client: We want a twenty acre parcel of ground zoned for animals.

Agent: Oh, you want a really isolated parcel away from everything.

Client: Well, it has to be close enough to the schools that our children will need to attend.

Agent: Oh, your children are of school age?

Client: Oh yes!

Agent: I bet they participate in a lot of school activities!

Client: Oh yes, Jennifer is the best little actress in the fourth grade and Tommy made the sixth grade basketball team last year.

Agent: Sounds like you'll be doing a fair bit of driving back and forth?

Client: I hope not—we have only one car now, but we'll probably get another one.

Agent: Well, you must both have farming backgrounds to be looking for a parcel like this.

Client: Well, actually we were both born and raised in Los Angeles, and have never lived anywhere else, but the idea sounds good.

Agent: You really love horses do you?

Client: Well, we have never actually had a horse but I rode one once at the state fair.

Agent: I see, and you said that you had $75,000 in your savings account to put down?

Client: Well, our Uncle Jake said that if we found a place we really liked he would consider lending us $60,000. We have $15,000 in our own bank account.

I could continue with this example for several more pages but I think you get the idea. The technique used by the agent was simple: he repeated back to the client in the form of a question what the client had just said to the agent. This acknowledged the client's statement and gave the client the opportunity to expand on an explanation. Most people, if given this opportunity will take it and provide far more information than you will get by direct questioning. If the agent who lost the sale had proceeded in the above manner, he would probably have shown the prospective clients property more suited to their real needs and wants.

The first requirement of listening is to close your mouth. The second requirement is to deliberately tell yourself that what you are thinking and what you have to say can wait. And lastly, you must participate in the other person's conversation. Not your conversation, not your agenda, but theirs. Successful people are good listeners, and because of it they are able to get to the heart of matters and to the real issues far more quickly and with far fewer bruises than others who fail to discover the real meanings and items of interest to those with whom they are dealing. Far more opportunities are gained by listening than by talking, and you probably already know that the people you consider great conversationalists are usually the ones who listen the most carefully to what you have to say.

Rule 10

> *Woe Is Me. What to Do? What to Do?*

Solving Problems—When, Where and How

This brief discussion is about problems and what to do about them. I'm not speaking about a specific problem or even a specific type of problem, but, inasmuch as this little book is primarily concerned with financial matters, the discussion can be in monetary terms. In a broader sense however, our research has shown that financially successful people handle most of the problems in their life in much the same way they handle financial dilemmas. I suspect the comments made here are valid for dealing with a wide spectrum of problems and not just those having to do with money. Perhaps the single most common characteristic of how financially adept people deal with problems can be expressed in one word—*now*.

They take care of problems as soon as possible, rather than allowing them to fester and grow. Whenever I think back upon a financial difficulty or dilemma it is clear that I could have minimized the damage had I acted sooner. Note that I am not saying that quick action always leads to the most brilliant solution. If timeliness was not an issue we could no doubt come up with a better solution than the one decided upon when we acted quickly. But problems have a tendency to grow appendages if left alone—one thing leads to another and the problem begins to grow more and more heads. The faster we try to cut one off, the more quickly it is replaced by two more. On the other hand, if problems are dealt with quickly and decisively they often do go away before any further incidental damage is done.

The classic example of this, of course, is a business dispute between you and a partner, between you and a supplier, or between you and a lender. Typically, the principals begin discussions and, if they arrive at a quick solution, the matter ends there. If, however, nothing is done and no decision is reached, at some point attorneys, collection agencies, and other intermediaries become involved. Once this happens, and particularly once attorneys get involved, things inevitably deteriorate, especially since attorneys have no real interest in solving their clients' problems; they can keep the meter running by dragging out the negotiations.

One of the most frustrating expenditures is a payment to your attorney which rivals the amount the dispute was over in the first place. Unless you are the sort of person who would rather argue than win, it is almost always cheaper to settle differences before intermediaries become involved. I'm certainly not suggesting that you give in or concede every time a dispute arises. I am suggesting that you deal with the problem immediately before it gains its own inexplicable momentum and inevitably winds up costing more. The latter is true whether you ultimately win or lose the dispute. Much as we would prefer not to admit it, most problems don't just go away.

They may enter a period of remission, but they have a tendency to come back to life at the most inopportune times. There is an old saying that a bad settlement is better than a good trial. While I'm not in complete agreement with that point of view, it is clear to me that money and time are better spent directly solving a problem than upon legal maneuvers and buying time.

I can relate from experience that every problem I have confronted immediately has been settled on more favorable terms than almost every problem I have ignored, drawn out, or put off. Highly successful people have confirmed this belief and told me that it takes considerably less time to settle matters immediately than it does when coping with the problems that have been postponed.

One particular aspect of this discussion should be expanded. No matter how financially successful you have been, there may come a time in your career when a payment to a creditor is due and, for one reason or another, you are short of cash and unable to meet the due date. Unfortunately, the typical response of debtors in this situation is to ignore the creditor and hope that he isn't paying attention, is too busy to take action, or (the real long shot) will believe that the money will come along before too long.

Each time the debtor's phone rings, someone different answers and the manager avoids any direct conversation with the creditor. This course of action may be the worst possible, because most often the creditor is not half as bad a guy as the debtor thinks he is. Furthermore, in most cases, the creditor's primary concern is the overall security of his money and not so much the punctuality of the payments. (Creditors will become agitated by habitually late payments, but there are other considerations which determine the position they will take.)

If the loan itself is not in jeopardy, creditors are usually willing to work with borrowers, so long—and I emphasize this—as borrowers are honest and keep the creditor informed of the situation. I can think of nothing which causes a creditor to take drastic action more quickly than the belief that he may never be repaid. And I can think of nothing to foster that belief more quickly than being ignored by the borrower. The advice is simple: if you have problems making a payment, call your creditor before the payment is due and explain matters. Normally, as long as it doesn't become a habit, creditors are usually cooperative. As someone once said, neither our worst fears nor greatest hopes are often realized.

In summary then, try to solve problems before they become serious. They aren't like wine, they don't become better with age. As added points of interest, keep in mind that we have a tendency to see problems only from our own perspective, and we have a further tendency to view the *other side* as having a stronger position than our own. In fact, the problem that exists may be more serious for the other side than for you. Consequently, a perfectly acceptable settlement may be easy to achieve if you act quickly.

For example, if you owe money to a plumbing contractor and don't pay his bill, you could be jeopardizing the continuation of that contractor's business; particularly if he, in turn, owes money to a supplier. If it reaches that stage he may sue, not only for the amount owed but additional damages caused by the refusal of his supplier to continue to provide raw materials. If the contractor had been called and your problem explained, he may have asked you to pay only one-third immediately so he could pay his supplier. An arrangement such as this could allow both his business and yours to live to profit another day.

Some problems can't be solved quickly and some problems are never solved satisfactorily, but characteristically, productive people confront their problems straight on, without delay, to at least evaluate their alternatives.

Rule 11

My Lawyer Can Beat Up Your Lawyer

Win - Win or Intimidation

The debate has been going on seemingly forever—which business philosophy is best? Some argue that everyone involved in a deal has to win and that deals which create losers are short-sighted and often come back to haunt the *winner*. Others argue that your only responsibility is to yourself, and that, by definition, every deal has a winner and a loser. Further, they say it's okay to use any legal means at your disposal to intimidate your opposition, so long as the most profitable deal is made. (They consider everyone else the opposition.)

Most business people who have been successful for a long time—not just a one deal killing—will recognize that financial dealings are often contests and that some participants will come out better than others. By the same token, they understand that there are advantages in being able to do repeat business, and that making enemies can cost dearly in the future.

Solving this dilemma is not as difficult as it might seem, once you recognize that each business or financial transaction has a certain *bundle of benefits* which all the participants get to share.

A _____ B

Benefits

Look at the example above—the area between Mr. A and Mr. B are the *goodies*, the profits, the benefits of any particular transaction. When the deal is done the final results could look like this:

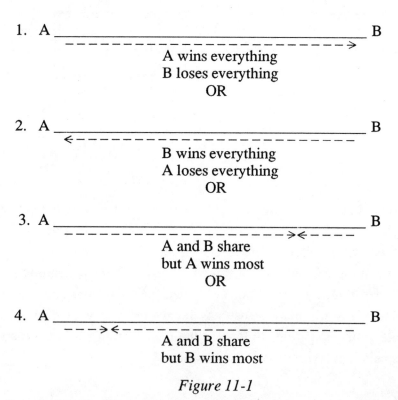

1. A _____ B

A wins everything
B loses everything
OR

2. A _____ B

B wins everything
A loses everything
OR

3. A _____ B

A and B share
but A wins most
OR

4. A _____ B

A and B share
but B wins most

Figure 11-1

The point is that 3 and 4 above are win-win solutions within a competitive framework. If you were Mr. A, example 3 is the type of end-result you would prefer. You win (earn) the majority of the pot, but B also winds up better than he started, which should induce B to do business with Mr. A again. Furthermore, even if B did not do an especially good job, no one wants to feel that they failed. This solution gives B a face-saving result, he gets some of the benefits. It is usually a mistake to wipe out the other guy; grudges can last a long time. Also, it's usually unnecessary. You can have the best of all worlds by aggressively going after your share of the total benefits while paying attention to the other side's ultimate position and recognizing that when both sides have a potential gain, the deal is more likely to close.

In short, the win-win strategy is best. This doesn't mean that all parties share the benefits equally, but that each party ends up better than they began. The best money makers keep an eye on their profits as well as what they believe to be the profits of the other side. Everybody can be a winner, even if some win more than others. That's the best deal.

Rule 12

> *Use Professionals, Even if They Aren't Relatives
> and You Have to Pay Them*

Experts—When and How to Use Them

A few years ago we were getting ready to build a motel in a small town and wanted to purchase a particular piece of ground. As part of the deal, we wanted the sellers of the property to carry the loan on which we would make monthly payments, including interest which was then two to three points higher than savings and loans were paying on deposits. Additionally, we wanted the sellers to subordinate their note to a new construction loan. In other words, we wanted them to give us the deed to

63

the property in exchange for us giving them an IOU secured by the property in second position (what would commonly be called a second mortgage).

I assigned one of my representatives to try and make the deal and after several months he still had no success, I finally asked him to tell me as much as he could about the sellers. He informed me that they were an elderly couple in their seventies who owned the land free and clear and had owned it for probably thirty-five years. The problem was apparent.

This elderly couple was concerned about the security of our note to them. They knew that if they sold the property and received cash they could put it into the savings bank and feel confident that it was insured and safe. No amount of persuasion by my representative would convince them that we were just as safe as the savings bank. It was clear that the more we tried to convince them of our financial stability and good intentions, the more it would come across as a hard sell, and the less inclined they would be to accept our offer.

Finally, I went to our banker and asked if he knew their banker. As luck would have it, he did, and I asked if he would call the seller's banker to convey, on a personal basis, information that would convince the seller's banker that we were financially sound and would make the payments as promised. Soon after that the sellers contacted us and said that, while they would not carry quite as much as we wanted, if we could give them another $10,000 in cash up front, they would do everything we asked with the balance.

The point of this little tale is credibility and who has it. The fact is that credibility doesn't always follow logical patterns. You may be the most honest person on earth, but if you are in a dispute with another party, their attorney will never believe you, but if your attorney gives their attorney the same information, it is more likely to be accepted. Call it professional courtesy or professional greed or the *I'll rub your back if you'll rub mine* approach. Your attorney will always do better with the other side's attorney than you will.

Your doctor will be able to make an appointment for you, with a specialist, more quickly than you can get one for yourself. Your CPA will do better at an IRS audit than you will alone, not because the CPA necessarily knows more than you, but because, in most professions there is some degree of professional courtesy. More importantly, it is often easier to deal with the other side's intermediary than with the other side directly. If concessions need to be made, there is less loss of face making them through an intermediary. When a tough stand is required it is easier to offend the intermediary than the principals because they come and go; but you may have to deal with that principal again in the future.

On one hand, it is easy to waste a lot of money on so-called experts; hourly fees often range well above one hundred dollars and I know of no expert who guarantees the results or agrees to return his fee if things don't work out.

Nevertheless, the selective use of experts or professionals is often an efficient way of settling problems or getting necessary information. It has been said that information about your competitor's engineering department can best be obtained by having your accountant talk to their accountant, he will tell your accountant everything that is wrong with the engineering department. The important point to remember is that unless the professional you hire is capable of doing the job, the benefits derived will be minimal and may, in fact, cause more harm than good. Don't skimp on hiring quality people. The best way to ensure that quality, is to check their references.

Also, remember that the experts are probably capable of performing a rather limited number of tasks efficiently. Generalists who claim to be able to handle accounting, contracts, and finance, probably don't do any of them very well. You are better served by paying a little more to the best available, making it clear that you are paying full price because you expect satisfactory results. This doesn't guarantee success, but at least it puts the expert on notice that you are demanding performance.

Keep in mind, however, that the ultimate responsibility is yours and it is your job to monitor what the expert is doing, even if you don't fully understand some of the technical details. People who make a lot of money usually adopt the attitude that what happens is their responsibility, regardless of who they have hired to take that responsibility.

One of my ex-partners had the attitude that everything that happened to him, good or bad, was his fault. In a clearly analytical sense this wasn't true. If our bookkeeper made an error the direct fault lay with her but, by taking the point of view that it was his fault, he took upon himself the responsibility of helping the bookkeeper so that her mistakes were minimized. Try it, it works.

The worst mistake, from my point of view, is turning problems over to attorneys and asking them to work it out. Several books have recently been published discussing ways of dealing with attorneys. The one thing they all have in common is that attorneys have no incentive for settling anything. They are usually paid by the hour, and their ego is often involved in drawing out and complicating problems that could be solved more quickly and more directly.

It has been my very clear experience that while our attorney is useful for legal advice and often contributes something significant to a *team effort*, attorneys are not necessarily better businessmen and are almost always worse negotiators than the people they represent. The lawyers usually become involved because of a breakdown in communication between parties and, once the attorneys are involved, a settlement becomes significantly more difficult to come by.

Don't be afraid to call your adversary and suggest another direct meeting directly with him, even though you are both represented by attorneys. If the other side is bright and serious they are probably no more anxious to spend more on attorney's fees than you are. Explain that you would like a meeting, notwithstanding any personal feelings, for the purpose of hashing out your problem. Most times they will accept and the meeting will be successful.

The attorneys can then come in and draw up a binding agreement based on the settlement between the principals. Stated differently, bringing in an attorney, or a CPA, or a financial advisor, does not mean turning things over to them. It is your money, your life, your time, and most of all, your responsibility. The experts can help, but they are never quite as interested or as serious about matters as the principals.

Conclusion

> *There Are No Heroes at Three O'Clock in the Morning*
> **Napoleon**

The preceding pages have discussed a number of related but separate *rules* for attaining and maintaining financial goals and objectives. Fair questions at this point are "What now?" and "How do I get started?"

Some time ago an acquaintance contemplated getting a college degree after having been in the work force for several years. He concluded that he *really* needed a degree to advance, but his most often-voiced argument was that going to school on a part time basis would take six to seven years to finish. Finally, a friend told him that the six or seven years would *pass* regardless of whether or not he returned to school. His only real choice was deciding if he would have a degree at the end of that time.

The same applies to your financial plans and aspirations. Time will pass whether or not you take stock of your current situation and adopt a plan of action to move forward. Let's consider some of the steps and decisions necessary to get started.

1. What do you really want to do?

Most of us know in our hearts what we would like to do, but for a variety of reasons we plod along doing something else. So first, admit *out loud* that you do have a dream and begin to take it seriously. I know that you may have a family and can't quit your job because the kids are in the habit of eating. But a lot of others who achieved their goals were once in the same position. If they were able to do it, so can you.

2. Research and plan.

One of the most common errors after making a commitment, is jumping headlong into it with all the necessary enthusiasm but none of the direction. People who have waited years before doing anything are suddenly without any patience whatsoever. It's as if the dreams will die unless they are consumed with activity. Look, researching and planning *count as doing something*! If you've been dreaming for ten years, six-months of research and planning isn't much more time and it will increase your odds of success. There are limits of course, and no matter how much planning you do there will always be loose ends, fears, and *three o'clocks in the mornings* when you know that it can't work. Fortunately, seven A.M. will come and with it a renewal of your spirit.

Write down your ideas and plans. I repeat, *write them down*, and don't worry about literary style—no one cares. The purpose of this is to force consideration of the logic of your ideas, and come to grips with possible problems. Furthermore, trusted advisors can more easily respond to a written plan than to a rambling conversation. Remember our discussion of how to get a loan? You will eventually need a written plan, and this is the best time to get it started.

By the way, expect negative comments from those with whom you discuss the plan, especially those closest to you. It's amazing how some people seem to feel almost obligated to put a damper on your emotions. Pay attention to legitimate comments that deal with the substance of your plan and discount the negative (envious?) snipes that can so easily bruise egos and destroy enthusiasm. Every successful person has had to endure disappointments, setbacks and problems and so will you. Plan and re-plan, write and rewrite. Finally it's time to end the planning phase and begin to put the plan into action, but first ...

3. Does the final plan even remotely resemble what you started out to do?

You had an idea which was really exciting and you've spent the necessary time researching, planning, *changing* and *modifying*. That's good, but have you changed and modified the excitement right out of the idea.

I was once involved with an investment group whose idea was to provide low cost, affordable housing in a blue collar community. The goal was a manufactured house which would sell for $49,000. As we researched and planned, it was decided that such things as dishwashers, redwood decks, two car garages, and a host of other features, were irresistible to prospective buyers. We also got greedy. The homes were put on postage-sized lots to increase the number of saleable homes. By the time the development was completed, our affordable home was around $70,000 on a twiggy-sized lot and the development was a dismal failure.

Was our idea bad? No, but the execution was terrible. We got so far from the original good idea that we essentially obliterated the best parts of it. The idea and the dream have to survive its implementation.

4. Get started.

Full time if your plan has devised a way to do it, or part-time if circumstances demand it. Either way, enthusiasm and the pleasure of doing what you most enjoy will be your key to success and prosperity whether you work for yourself or a large corporation. You'll wonder why you didn't do it years ago. Best of Luck.

Notes

Notes

Order Form

Thank you for purchasing *Twelve Rules for Getting Rich*. To order additional copies of this book or those described below, please complete the order form or telephone **1-800-SLAWSON.**

The Formula for Successful Marketing
The Complete Guide for Marketing Professionals

Managing Your Money
A Lifetime Strategy for Financial Independence

Name _____

Address _____

City_____ State _____ Zip _____

Qty.	Title	Price ea.	Total
	Twelve Rules for Getting Rich	$8.95	
	The Formula for Successful Marketing	$8.95	
	Managing Your Money	$8.95	

U.S. SHIPPING Books are shipped UPS except where a post office is given as a delivery address.	Subtotal
	Sales Tax: CA residents add 7.25%
	Shipping & Handling: $3.00 for first book, 50 cents for each additional book.
	TOTAL

FORM OF PAYMENT

☐ Visa ☐ MasterCard ☐ Check

Card #: ⎢ ⎢ ⎢ ⎢ ⎢ ⎢ ⎢ ⎢ ⎢ ⎢ ⎢ ⎢ ⎢ ⎢ ⎢

Expiration Date: _____

Signature: _____

Mail this order form to:

Avant Books®
Slawson Communications, Inc.
165 Vallecitos de Oro
San Marcos, CA 92069-1436

(619) 744-2299